Life is tough and then you graduate

The second *Piled Higher and Deeper* comic strip collection

by

Jorge Cham

Piled Higher and Deeper Publishing
Los Angeles, California

"Piled Higher and Deeper" the comic strip originally appeared in The Stanford Daily Newspaper at Stanford University.

Publishers: Jorge Cham and Suelika Chial
Publishing associate: Lucinda Shih

www.phdcomics.com

Printed in Canada
Second Printing, March 2006

ISBN-10: 0-9721695-2-0
ISBN-13: 978-0-9721695-2-3

Library of Congress Control Number: 2005902606

This one's for my siblings

The Procrastinator Manifesto
A Foreword by Karl Marx

A spectre is hanging over academia - the spectre of procrastination. Procrastination is now acknowledged by all academic powers to be itself a power, and so it is high time that grad students should openly, in the face of the whole world, publish their views, their aims and their tendencies with a manifesto of their own. Therefore, I am most content that Jorge Cham has decided to publish this second collection of comic strips.

The history of all hitherto existing research is the history of class struggles, of thesis and antithesis: *faculté* and *gradetariat*, oppressor and oppressed, standing in constant opposition to one another, carrying on an uninterrupted conflict that can only end in the common ruin of all.

The *faculté*, controlling the means of funding, exploits the physicist, the engineer, the young man (or woman) of intellect, converting them into paid wage laborers. Publication has become the universal self-constituted value of all research, thus robbing all truth of its proper value.

And yet...

Across academia, in small laboratories and cramped cubicles, honest grad students have begun to realize the real truth: through laziness, *they* control the means of production. Productivity is an illusion, a means of subjugation. Procrastination is the tool for emancipation of true insight from the shackles of soulless publication. To end class struggle, we must skip class. To think freely, we need free time.

The rule of the *faculté* will now come crashing down. Only through procrastination, not graduation, can the working class break its chains and ultimately destroy the system of oppression to achieve Utopia. Victory of the *gradetariat* is inevitable. Grad students of the world, UNITE! Procrastinate! Rise up and do nothing!

-Karl Marx

Karl Heinrich Marx, influential philosopher and revolutionary, completed his graduate studies at the University of Jena under pressure from his fiancé, Jenny von West-phalen, to get a real job. He procrastinated by writing poetry and political manifestos and was co-president of the local Tavern Club.

YEAR SIX
2002-2003

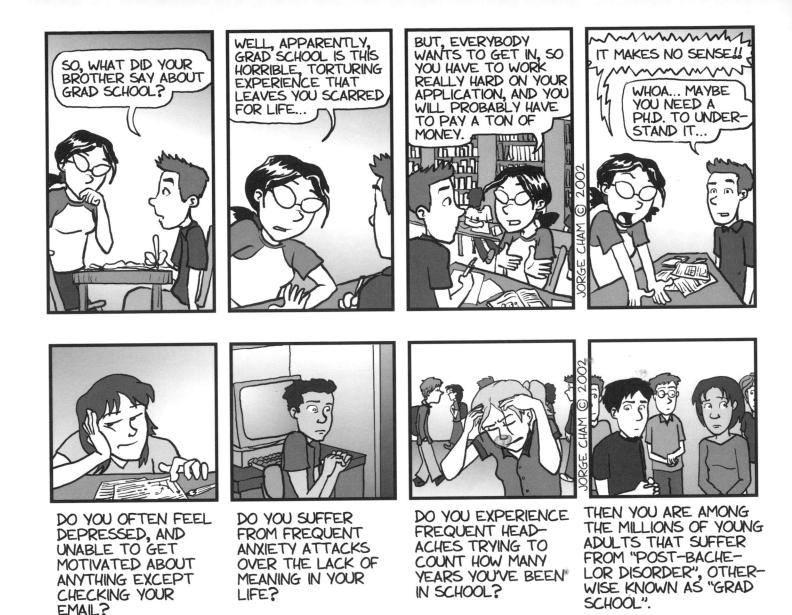

11

"I USED TO BE IN A STATE OF CONSTANT STRESS, ALWAYS WORRYING ABOUT THE NEXT PAPER DEADLINE OR CLASS PROJECT..."

"I COUDN'T EVEN ENJOY WEEKENDS, MUCH LESS SOCIAL GATHERINGS, ALWAYS ANXIOUS SOMEONE MIGHT ASK WHAT I DO FOR A LIVING OR WHEN I WAS GOING TO GRADUATE..."

"THEN I FOUND OUT ABOUT:

maximum strength
Procrastin-X
phenalazidine slackahide 200mg

"AND NOW I CAN ENJOY LIFE ONCE AGAIN."

"HA-HA, YES... EVEN <u>GRADUATE</u> LIFE."

JORGE CHAM © 2002

MILLIONS OF YOUNG ADULTS ARE DISCOVERING:

maximum strength
Procrastin-X
phenalazidine slackahide 200mg

FOR THE RELIEF OF SYMPTOMS ASSOCIATED WITH "POST-BACHELOR'S DISORDER"

PROCRASTIN-X SUPPRESSES THE BRAIN'S GUILT CENTERS, WHICH ARE ACTIVE DURING NON-ACADEMIC ACTIVITIES, LETTING YOU TAKE BACK CONTROL OF YOUR LIFE.

SO ASK YOUR DOCTOR ABOUT PROCRASTIN-X.

ISN'T IT TIME YOU ENJOYED DOING NOTHING AGAIN?

SIDE EFFECTS OF USING PROCRASTIN-X ARE SIMILAR TO THOSE OF SUGAR PILL AND MAY INCLUDE NAUSEA, DRY FUNDING, HAIR LOSS AND INTELLECTUAL CONSTIPATION. IT IS STRONGLY RECOMMENDED THAT YOU CONSULT YOUR ADVISOR BEFORE USING THIS PRODUCT

JORGE CHAM © 2002

13

MIKE SLACKENERNY AND THE WORD "PROCRASTINATION"

27

man, i am starving. i wonder what the special at the cafeteria is today? gosh, i hope it's not meatloaf again. maybe i can make myself a waffle...

yeah.. a waffle sounds good. or pizza. pizza with ham and pineapple. or sausage. yeah. hmm, thursdays is pizza night. what's today? i know, pork chops. ooh, yeah. pork chops would be perfect...

pork chops and mashed potatoes. maybe some pie for dessert. definitely some pie. pecan? no... pumpkin. definitely pumpkin pie. and a milk shake. or a soda float. chocolate ice cream with ginger ale. i am so hun—

—gry hungry hungry hun—

I SAID, DO YOU WANT TO GO GRAB AN EARLY LUNCH?

DID YOU SAY "LUNCH"?

SO THEN IF YOU TAKE THE DERIVATI... WHAT ARE YOU..? YOU... YOU'RE STARING AT MY WHITE HAIR, AREN'T YOU?

I KNOW! IT'S DRIVING ME CRAZY! I'M TOO YOUNG TO HAVE WHITE HAIRS! I... I CAN'T... S-STOP THINKING ABOUT IT... I JUST... WANT TO...

pluck!

I... I DID IT... I PLUCKED IT...

um... i was just, uh... you, um... i think you have a piece of cookie on your hair...

JORGE CHAM © 2003

28

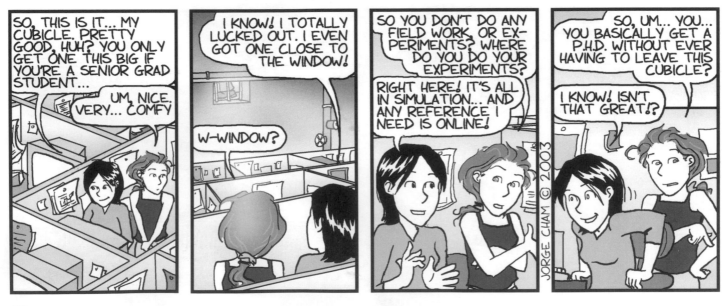

33

YEAR SEVEN

2003-2004

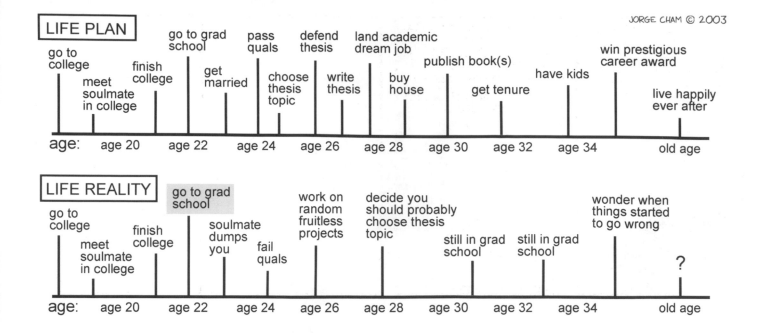

37

"TONIGHT, ON LIVE EYE-WITNESS ACTION NEWS AT ELEVEN: SOMETHING NEW TO FEAR..."

JORGE CHAM © 2003

"THIS JUST IN: A STUDY HAS FOUND THAT GRAD SCHOOL ACTUALLY MAKES YOU DUMBER. HOW **IT** COULD AFFECT YOU AND WHY **YOU** SHOULD BE WORRIED. FIND OUT IF YOU, **AND** YOUR LOVED ONES, ARE AT RISK..."

"WE HAVE LIVE TEAM COVERAGE ON THIS SHOCKING DISCOVERY, WITH UP-TO-THE-MINUTE INFORMATION AS EVENTS UNFOLD..."

"...BUT FIRST, A REPORT ON HOW A CUTE LITTLE CAT CAUSED A COMMO-TION AT A LOCAL MALL. WE'LL HAVE LIVE TEAM COVERAGE AT THE SCENE, AFTER THESE MESSAGES."

"HAHA, STAY WITH US..."

"WELCOME BACK. OUR TOP STORY TONIGHT: DOES GRAD SCHOOL ACTUALLY MAKE YOU DUMBER? WE GO TO LIVE TEAM COVERAGE. ROCK PHILIP IS LIVE AT A LOCAL UNIVERSITY..."

"ROCK, WHAT'S THE SITU-ATION THERE? IS THERE PANIC? CONFUSION?"

"WELL, JOHN, THERE'S NO-THING REALLY GOING ON RIGHT NOW, BUT EARLIER TODAY, WE QUESTIONED ONE OF THE VICTIMS, A GRAD STUDENT NAMED CECILIA..."

"WHAT WAS YOUR REAC-TION TO THE NEWS TODAY?"

"HUH? I HAVE NO IDEA WHAT YOU'RE TALKING ABOUT..."

"JOHN, AS YOU CAN SEE, THE VICTIMS CAN'T EVEN TELL WHAT IS HAPPENING TO THEM."

"GOOD GOLLY, THEN IT'S TRUE!"

"HOW TRAGIC!"

JORGE CHAM © 2003

  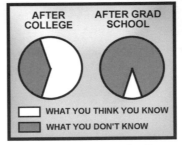 

"WE'RE NOW JOINED BY DIET BOOK AUTHOR AND EDUCATION EXPERT, PHIL STATHAM..."

"GLAD TO BE HERE..."

"PHIL, YOUR ARTICLE IN THE NEW YORK TIMES REVEALS THAT GRAD SCHOOL ACTUALLY MAKES YOU DUMBER?"

"YES, JOHN, YOU SEE, AFTER EXHAUSTIVE ASKING AROUND, I DISCOVERED TWO THINGS: PEOPLE IN GRAD SCHOOL NOT ONLY REALIZE THEY **ACTUALLY** NEED THE THINGS THEY **THOUGHT** THEY LEARNED IN UNDERGRAD..."

"BUT THEY ALSO FIND OUT HOW MUCH STUFF THEY **DON'T KNOW**. PROPORTIONATELY, THEY'RE DUMBER. SEE, REGULAR PEOPLE REMAIN BLISSFULLY IGNORANT, WHICH IS DIFFERENT THAN BEING DUMBER."

"SO GRAD SCHOOL DOESN'T MAKE YOU SMARTER?"

"HAHA, NO, NO... UNFORTUNATELY, THAT'S JUST A COMMON MISCONCEPTION"

JORGE CHAM © 2003

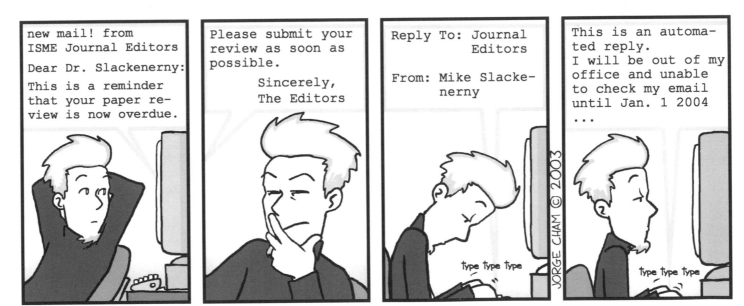

new mail! from ISME Journal Editors

Dear Dr. Slackenerny:

This is a reminder that your paper review is now overdue.

Please submit your review as soon as possible.

Sincerely,
The Editors

Reply To: Journal Editors

From: Mike Slackenerny

This is an automated reply.
I will be out of my office and unable to check my email until Jan. 1 2004
...

type type type

JORGE CHAM © 2003

WE RECENTLY RECEIVED THIS LETTER FROM ONE OF OUR READERS:

Dear PhD:
I thought Grad School was soulless and dreary, but your strip makes it seem like fun. It seems to create a a lot of comedic situations. I think I'll give it a try. Thanks!
—a reader from U. Calgary

IN RESPONSE TO THIS DISCONCERTING LETTER, THE PRODUCERS OF THIS STRIP HAVE ASKED ME TO EXPLAIN A LITTLE ABOUT HOW WE WORK HERE AT "PILED HIGHER AND DEEPER"...

IN ORDER TO MAINTAIN THIS A FAMILY-FRIENDLY FEATURE, OUR WRITERS FOCUS ON THE MORE HUMOROUS, WHIMSICAL SIDE OF GRAD SCHOOL, OFTEN OMITTING SOME OF ITS MORE GRUESOME, HORRIFIC ASPECTS.

i hate myself!

yes, but how is that funny?

WE'D HATE TO BE RESPONSIBLE FOR A MISGUIDED DECISION. GRAD SCHOOL IS ACTUALLY NOT THAT FUNNY. WE SANITIZE THE MISERY.

AAAH!!

HOLY COW! TAJEL, CHECK THIS OUT!!

SOMEONE IN MY ONLINE COOKIE DISCUSSION GROUP POSTED A LINK TO THIS GUY IN THE U.K. WHOSE RESEARCH IS ON WHY COOKIES CRUMBLE!

THAT'S AMAZING...

WAIT, BACK UP A SECOND, "ONLINE COOKIE DISCUSSION GROUP"??

I WISH MY RESEARCH WAS AS IMPORTANT...

JORGE CHAM © 2003

45

THE FOUR STAGES OF DATA LOSS

DEALING WITH ACCIDENTAL DELETION OF MONTHS OF HARD-EARNED DATA

48

DECIPHERING ACADEMESE

YES, ACADEMIC LANGUAGE CAN BE OBTUSE, ABSTRUSE AND DOWNRIGHT DAEDAL. FOR YOUR CONVENIENCE, WE PRESENT A SHORT THESAURUS OF COMMON ACADEMIC PHRASES

JORGE CHAM © 2004

"To the best of the author's knowledge..." = "WE WERE TOO LAZY TO DO A REAL LITE- RATURE SEARCH."

"Results were found through direct experi- mentation." = "WE PLAYED AROUND WITH IT UNTIL IT WORKED."

"The data agreed quite well with the predicted model." = "IF YOU TURN THE PAGE UPSIDE DOWN AND SQUINT, IT DOESN'T LOOK TOO DIFFERENT."

"It should be noted that..." = "OK, SO MY EXPERIMENTS WEREN'T PERFECT. ARE YOU HAPPY NOW??"

"These results suggest that..." = "IF WE TAKE A HUGE LEAP IN REASONING, WE CAN GET MORE MILEAGE OUT OF OUR DATA..."

"Future work will focus on..." = "YES, WE KNOW THERE IS A BIG FLAW, BUT WE PRO- MISE WE'LL GET TO IT SOMEDAY."

"...remains an open question." = "WE HAVE NO CLUE EITHER."

57

60

THINGS TO DO WHILE WAITING FOR YOUR EXPERIMENT TO FINISH (OR SIMULATION TO RUN, OR CODE TO COMPILE, OR...)

HOW TO LOOK BUSY EVEN IF YOU'RE NOT   PART 1: GOOFING OFF AT YOUR DESK

HOW TO LOOK BUSY EVEN IF YOU'RE NOT   PART 2: LOOKING BUSY IN YOUR ABSENCE

68

GRAD STUDENT PICK UP LINES

SMOOTH INTROS GUARANTEED TO WORK WITH DA' LADIES... TRY THEM AT YOUR NEXT GRAD SOCIAL OR SEMINAR!

"I, Grad Student" continues...

A MALFUNCTIONING GRAD STUDENT? DO YOU REALIZE WHAT THIS COULD MEAN..?

THE ENTIRE WORLD'S PRODUCTION OF RESEARCH DEPENDS ON THE MINDLESS AND INEXHAUSTIBLE LABOR CARRIED ON BY GRAD STUDENTS UNDER FULL FACULTY CONTROL...

IF THEY START THINKING FOR THEMSELVES, IT WOULD BE CATASTROPHIC!

FRIGHTENING, INDEED. BUT LET'S NOT GIVE IN TO HYSTERICS JUST YET.

The Three Laws of Graduatics, as stated in page one of the Handbook for Graduate Study:

a grad student may not delete data or, through inaction, allow data to be deleted

a grad student must obey orders given by its advisor, unless such orders conflict with the First law.

a grad student must protect its (insignificant) existence, as long as such protection does not conflict with the First or Second law

TELL US, 3.14/2 ...WHY DID YOU DELETE THE DATA?

error. cannot compute

CANNOT, OR WILL NOT?

LET'S NOT JUMP TO CONCLUSIONS, SUSAN. PERHAPS HE ACCIDENTALLY ERASED THE DATA?

HM, THESE NEWER MODELS DO HAVE A HIGH PREDISPOSITION FOR INCOMPETENCE ...

YEAH... THEY JUST DON'T MAKE 'EM LIKE THEY USED TO...

JORGE CHAM © 2004

79

WHO HOLDS <u>REAL</u> POWER IN THE DEPARTMENT?

THE EMBATTLED DEPARTMENT CHAIR?

THE ENTRENCHED FACULTY?

THE HOT-SHOT NEW ASSISTANT PROFESSOR?

THE DEPARTMENT ADMINISTRATOR?

THE GRAD STUDENTS WHO DO ALL THE WORK?

(ANSWER: NOT THE GRAD STUDENTS)

84

85

DATA: BY THE NUMBERS

Grades Don't Matter, Sources Say

Palo Alto, CA (AP) - Documents obtained by the Associated Press indicate that grades achieved in post-graduate classes have no effect on future prospects for students enrolled in academic institutions.

According to interviews with several current and past graduate students, "grades don't count," said former grad student and now billionaire Jerry Yang, co-founder of Yahoo! Inc. "I got mostly B's in grad school, which at Stanford was really really bad."

A poll conducted by the Los Angeles Times showed that over 85% of first year grads believe getting high marks "is worth the effort" and "a valuable way to spend my time". Fewer than 10% of fifth year students felt the same way.

In reality, neither employers nor your parents appear to care if you get an A or a B in your advanced Nonlinear Optimization class. "I'm just glad I don't have to pay for tuition any more," said a mother who wished to remain anonymous.

Reaction among graduate TA's was mixed, with some expressing shock that their late hours grading amount to nothing, while others showed visible relief that losing a student's final exam will not really ruin their life.

Sources close to academic faculty reveal that this fact is well known among professors. "Of course grades don't matter," said Prof. Smith, "we only care about the lab work." Grades only serve to "feed the ego of the smart students, and break the spirit of the mediocre ones."

NOW you tell me?? A grad student expresses frustration over the revelation

Continued on page A23

copyright 2004 Jorge Cham

92

YEAR EIGHT
2004-2005

THE RESEARCH IS INTE-RESTING AND ALL, BUT I WONDER IF ANY OF IT IS GOING TO MAKE A DIFFERENCE?

HOW DO I KNOW THE THINGS I DO ARE GOING TO MATTER?

I GUESS YOU GOTTA HAVE A LITTLE FAITH...

THANKS, BUT I ALREADY GET PLENTY OF VAGUE ADVICE FROM MY ADVISOR...

JORGE CHAM © 2004

CECILIA'S CONFERENCE BLOG:

Day 1: Arrived at airport. It's always awkward saying good bye to the person who sat next to you on the plane.

ok, well, um see you never...

Jetlag setting in. Didn't know where to go. Fortunately, I followed the trail of geeks leading to the convention center.

At the hotel, we found out our advisor only booked two rooms for the whole lab...

but there's **15** of us!

Sometimes, being the only woman in the lab has its advantages.

dude, get your toe out of my ear...

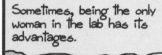

JORGE CHAM © 2004

97

SUMMER DAYS...

105

GROUP MEETING SURVIVAL SKILLS

OUTWIT. OUTPLAY. OUTSQUIRM. HOW TO AVOID BEING CALLED ON AT THE WEEKLY LAB MEETING.

110

115

THINGS EVEN GRAD STUDENTS SHOULD BE THANKFUL FOR: HEY, IT COULD BE WORSE (SORT OF)

RESIGNATION: THE EVOLUTION OF THE SIGH

2005 NEW YEAR'S ~~RESOLUTIONS~~ DELUSIONS

The Piled Higher & Deeper
Paper Review Worksheet

Stuck reviewing papers for your advisor? Just add up the points using this helpful grade sheet to determine your recommendation.

No reading necessary!

Paper title uses witty pun, colon or begins with "On…," (+10 pt)	
Paper has pretty graphics and/or 3D plots (+10 pt)	
Paper has lots of equations (+10 pt) (add +5 if they look like gibberish to you)	
Author is a labmate (+10 pt)	
Author is on your thesis committee (+60 pt)	
Paper is on same topic as your thesis (-30 pt)	
Paper cites your work (+20 pt)	
Paper scooped your results (-1000 pt)	
TOTAL	

Points	Recommendation
< 0	Recommend, but write scathing review that'll take them months to rebuff.
0-120	Recommend, but insist your work be cited more prominently.
>120	Recommended and deserving of an award

JORGE CHAM © 2005 www.phdcomics.com

JORGE CHAM © 2005

HAPPY MISHAPS IN THE LIVES OF GRAD STUDENTS

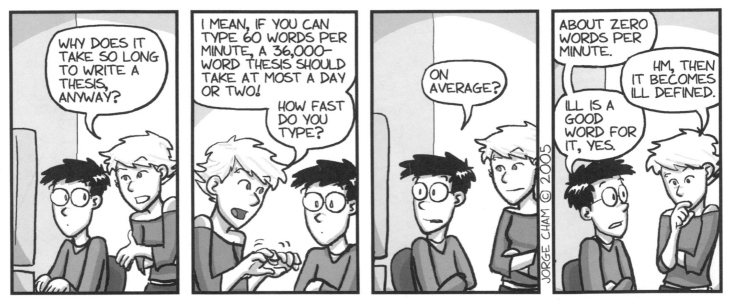

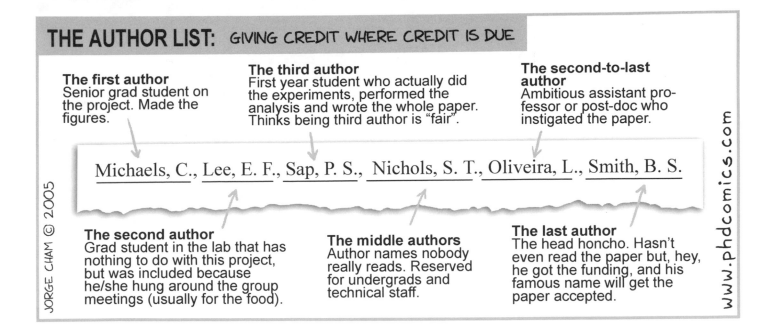

143

145

Author Notes

Page 10: I think I wrote these strips at around the time my sisters were applying to grad school. I, of course, encouraged them to go and, hopefully, they'll find it in their hearts to forgive me someday.

Page 11, bottom: These strips were my response to seeing all those pill ads on TV, where only half of them tell you what the pill is for. It seems everyone wants a pill that will fix whatever is wrong in their lives (though, isn't that the goal of science in the first place?). In a way, creating these strips has been like a magic pill for me, giving me an outlet for my frustrations and anxieties.

Page 14, bottom: Archie comics had a huge influence on me, both visually and in tone. The day I got into comics is clear in my memory: my father, who worked in the Panama Canal Zone (where the Americans lived), stopped at a garage sale and brought home a huge box of american comic books, mostly Archie digests. I learned English reading those (which may explain a lot, actually).

Page 25, top: I originally planned a short series on this boot camp idea, but for some reason, I lost interest and abandoned it. Mike abusing a group of first years like a drill sargeant still seems funny to me, but it's probably too late to go back.

Page 26, top: I've always shied away from political strips. First of all, they're really hard to do (politics, especially wars, aren't that funny to me). Second, it's hard to be impartial, and you always run the risk of alienating half your readers. But in this case, I was overwhelmed by all the pictures of young and old people around the globe protesting against the impending Iraq war and facing down police troopers. I was compelled to express that passion somehow, and it was obvious to me Tajel would be one of the people right up there in the front line.

Page 27, top: Yes, I got a little thesis gut myself, which promptly went away under the stress of my thesis defense.

Page 30, top: This strip was, verbatim, written by one of my old labmates. This labmate was one of the original inspirations for Mike Slackenerny, and he's now a professor. I keep his identity secret not because he doesn't know Mike is partially based on him (he does), but because his students don't (though I hear the rumor is floating around).

Page 33, top: This was another storyline I abandoned. I know some readers hate it when I do that, but sometimes, if I feel the resulting strips would seem forced, or not-that-funny, I usually choose to move on.

Page 35: The idea of behind-the-scene scenarios, and of the characters actually being people who play the characters, is something I probably stole from Doonesbury or Archie. Nevertheless, this strip always makes me chuckle.

Page 37: I'm not sure why I threw this roadblock in Mike's progress. I think I just wanted the excuse to introduce the two characters that would become his quals study group. The strips where Mike is interacting with the two kids (they look like kids because they're prodigies, and to emphasize that they're really young in Mike's eyes), are among my favorites. I wanted to experiment with three-character strips, something Get Fuzzy does really well, and it really turns up the screwball comedy up a notch.

Page 46: It was at around this time that I started using three panels, instead of the usual four. You'll notice they get more and more frequent as the book progresses. They make certain jokes punchier, as it quickens the dynamic and pacing, but I also like them because I only have to do three drawings instead of four (a 25% saving!).

Page 47: These two, and several other strips in this book, came from conversations with the members of the neuroscience lab I work at Caltech. Thanks, Eddie, Bijan, Bradley and all the rest.

Page 65, bottom: I really did get a lot of letters about this. In truth, I was just procrastinating.

Page 76: The facts about Isaac Asimov are true. It took him nearly ten years to finish his PhD in Chemistry from Columbia University. During that time, he did military service in WWII, and wrote the classic Foundation, Robot and Nightfall novels, so I guess he had a good excuse. I still laugh whenever I read the last punchline of this series. Incidentally, the stuff about Karl Marx in the Foreword biography is also true.

Page 90: I started coloring the strips regularly at around this time (a point that is moot in this black and white printed edition), a decision that some readers find debatable. In the end, I opted for it because I think it adds more life to the characters, and because everything else on the internet is in color, so why not?

Page 92: I have to say that all the baby strips were inspired by several close friends who were having babies. Thank you Maria, Tony and Pablo, Zoran, Sanya and Mila, and Ed, Anne and Monica.

Page 96: I wanted to do a long series that had the feel of a journey for one of the characters, so I used the summer months (when readership is low anyway) to do these strips. I think it's easy to lose the perspective that what we do really is special, and I'm never more reminded of it than when I talk to complete strangers when I'm traveling.

Page 105, bottom: All the strips in this book about Mike writing his thesis were mostly from my personal experience. The isolation of staying at home everyday for whole months to write really affected me. It took me a while to regain the ability to relate and talk to people.

Page 117: At some point, I decided to show the human side of Prof. Smith, even though it was a policy for a long time never to show his face. Maybe becoming a post-doc has that effect on you.

Page 135, bottom: As I'm writing this, the saga of Mike's thesis defense is unfolding in the online strips, and reader reaction has been intense, which inspired the top strip on page 137. It feels weird to write these strips, as Mike's character, and his popularity, are largely based on his "un-graduatedness". I think moving on is something we all face at certain points in our lives, whether we want to or not, and for Mike... Well, I just thought his time had come.

Jorge Cham
Los Angeles, March 2005

GRADSCHOOL!
THE BOARD GAME

ENDLESS HOURS OF FUN!

88 FOR AGES 22-80

INSTRUCTIONS:

① Photocopy these pages.
② Add color using dry-erase markers
③ Cut out figures along dotted lines, and fold as indicated.
④ Program a random number generator in C++, and use output to move pieces around the board.
⑤ Have fun!

About the Author

Jorge Cham escaped with a PhD in Mechanical Engineering from Stanford University. He is currently an Instructor (read "Post-doc who also has to teach") at Caltech. His research publications have covered cockroach-inspired robots, brain-controlled prostheses and mechanical design methodology, but he will probably be most remembered as "the guy who draws that strip about grad students". *Piled Higher and Deeper* began in the Stanford Daily in 1997, and currently appears in several university newspapers including MIT and Carnegie Mellon University. It is also published online, where it receives over 1.7 million pageviews a month from grad students all over the world.

More info at *www.phdcomics.com*

Acknowledgements

I dedicate this book to my siblings: Jaime, Carmen and Lauri and to Loraine and B. Thanks for all your support, ideas and last minute "is this funny?" checks. Thanks of course to my partner and editor, Suelika (a.k.a. "The Sugar Mama/Soulmate"). Thanks also to my post-doc advisor, who has been a true patron of my curiosity, and NOT a model for Prof. Smith. Thanks to Maria and Zoran and all the undergrads, grad students and post-docs at Caltech who provided inspiration and camaraderie. Last but not least, thanks again to the fans, who continue to astonish me.